WEEKLY TIME
SHEET LOG BOOK

_____

_____

_____

_____

Weekly Time Sheet

EMPLOYEE NAME:		WEEK ENDING:
DEPARTMENT:		EXEMPTIONS:

DAY OF WEEK	MORNING		AFTERNOON		OVERTIME		FOR OFFICE USE ONLY	
	IN	OUT	IN	OUT	IN	OUT	REGULAR HOURS	OVERTIME HOURS
MONDAY								
TUESDAY								
WEDNESDAY								
THURSDAY								
FRIDAY								
SATURDAY								
SUNDAY								
TOTAL HOURS								

OVERTIME
AUTHORIZATION_____

EMPLOYEE
SIGNATURE_____

This time sheet must be filled and signed by Employee Daily .
Overtime needs to be authorized by Authority First.

Weekly Time Sheet

EMPLOYEE NAME:	WEEK ENDING:
DEPARTMENT:	EXEMPTIONS:

DAY OF WEEK	MORNING		AFTERNOON		OVERTIME		FOR OFFICE USE ONLY	
	IN	OUT	IN	OUT	IN	OUT	REGULAR HOURS	OVERTIME HOURS
MONDAY								
TUESDAY								
WEDNESDAY								
THURSDAY								
FRIDAY								
SATURDAY								
SUNDAY								
TOTAL HOURS								

OVERTIME
AUTHORIZATION_____

EMPLOYEE
SIGNATURE_____

This time sheet must be filled and signed by Employee Daily .
Overtime needs to be authorized by Authority First.

Weekly Time Sheet

EMPLOYEE NAME:		WEEK ENDING:	
DEPARTMENT:		EXEMPTIONS:	

DAY OF WEEK	MORNING		AFTERNOON		OVERTIME		FOR OFFICE USE ONLY	
	IN	OUT	IN	OUT	IN	OUT	REGULAR HOURS	OVERTIME HOURS
MONDAY								
TUESDAY								
WEDNESDAY								
THURSDAY								
FRIDAY								
SATURDAY								
SUNDAY								
TOTAL HOURS								

OVERTIME
AUTHORIZATION_____

EMPLOYEE
SIGNATURE_____

This time sheet must be filled and signed by Employee Daily .
Overtime needs to be authorized by Authority First.

Weekly Time Sheet

EMPLOYEE NAME:	WEEK ENDING:
DEPARTMENT:	EXEMPTIONS:

DAY OF WEEK	MORNING		AFTERNOON		OVERTIME		FOR OFFICE USE ONLY	
	IN	OUT	IN	OUT	IN	OUT	REGULAR HOURS	OVERTIME HOURS
MONDAY								
TUESDAY								
WEDNESDAY								
THURSDAY								
FRIDAY								
SATURDAY								
SUNDAY								
TOTAL HOURS								

OVERTIME
AUTHORIZATION_____

EMPLOYEE
SIGNATURE_____

This time sheet must be filled and signed by Employee Daily .
Overtime needs to be authorized by Authority First.

Weekly Time Sheet

EMPLOYEE NAME:		WEEK ENDING:
DEPARTMENT:		EXEMPTIONS:

DAY OF WEEK	MORNING		AFTERNOON		OVERTIME		FOR OFFICE USE ONLY	
	IN	OUT	IN	OUT	IN	OUT	REGULAR HOURS	OVERTIME HOURS
MONDAY								
TUESDAY								
WEDNESDAY								
THURSDAY								
FRIDAY								
SATURDAY								
SUNDAY								
TOTAL HOURS								

OVERTIME AUTHORIZATION_____   EMPLOYEE SIGNATURE_____

This time sheet must be filled and signed by Employee Daily .
Overtime needs to be authorized by Authority First.

Weekly Time Sheet

EMPLOYEE NAME:	WEEK ENDING:
DEPARTMENT:	EXEMPTIONS:

DAY OF WEEK	MORNING		AFTERNOON		OVERTIME		FOR OFFICE USE ONLY	
	IN	OUT	IN	OUT	IN	OUT	REGULAR HOURS	OVERTIME HOURS
MONDAY								
TUESDAY								
WEDNESDAY								
THURSDAY								
FRIDAY								
SATURDAY								
SUNDAY								
TOTAL HOURS								

OVERTIME AUTHORIZATION_____

EMPLOYEE SIGNATURE_____

This time sheet must be filled and signed by Employee Daily .
Overtime needs to be authorized by Authority First.

Weekly Time Sheet

EMPLOYEE NAME:		WEEK ENDING:
DEPARTMENT:		EXEMPTIONS:

DAY OF WEEK	MORNING		AFTERNOON		OVERTIME		FOR OFFICE USE ONLY	
	IN	OUT	IN	OUT	IN	OUT	REGULAR HOURS	OVERTIME HOURS
MONDAY								
TUESDAY								
WEDNESDAY								
THURSDAY								
FRIDAY								
SATURDAY								
SUNDAY								
TOTAL HOURS								

OVERTIME AUTHORIZATION_____ **EMPLOYEE SIGNATURE**_____

This time sheet must be filled and signed by Employee Daily .
Overtime needs to be authorized by Authority First.

Weekly Time Sheet

EMPLOYEE NAME:		WEEK ENDING:
DEPARTMENT:		EXEMPTIONS:

DAY OF WEEK	MORNING		AFTERNOON		OVERTIME		FOR OFFICE USE ONLY	
	IN	OUT	IN	OUT	IN	OUT	REGULAR HOURS	OVERTIME HOURS
MONDAY								
TUESDAY								
WEDNESDAY								
THURSDAY								
FRIDAY								
SATURDAY								
SUNDAY								
TOTAL HOURS								

OVERTIME
AUTHORIZATION_____

EMPLOYEE
SIGNATURE_____

This time sheet must be filled and signed by Employee Daily .
Overtime needs to be authorized by Authority First.

Weekly Time Sheet

EMPLOYEE NAME:		WEEK ENDING:
DEPARTMENT:		EXEMPTIONS:

DAY OF WEEK	MORNING		AFTERNOON		OVERTIME		FOR OFFICE USE ONLY	
	IN	OUT	IN	OUT	IN	OUT	REGULAR HOURS	OVERTIME HOURS
MONDAY								
TUESDAY								
WEDNESDAY								
THURSDAY								
FRIDAY								
SATURDAY								
SUNDAY								
TOTAL HOURS								

OVERTIME
AUTHORIZATION_____

EMPLOYEE
SIGNATURE_____

This time sheet must be filled and signed by Employee Daily .
Overtime needs to be authorized by Authority First.

Weekly Time Sheet

EMPLOYEE NAME:	WEEK ENDING:
DEPARTMENT:	EXEMPTIONS:

DAY OF WEEK	MORNING		AFTERNOON		OVERTIME		FOR OFFICE USE ONLY	
	IN	OUT	IN	OUT	IN	OUT	REGULAR HOURS	OVERTIME HOURS
MONDAY								
TUESDAY								
WEDNESDAY								
THURSDAY								
FRIDAY								
SATURDAY								
SUNDAY								
TOTAL HOURS								

OVERTIME
AUTHORIZATION_____

EMPLOYEE
SIGNATURE_____

This time sheet must be filled and signed by Employee Daily .
Overtime needs to be authorized by Authority First.

Weekly Time Sheet

EMPLOYEE NAME:		WEEK ENDING:
DEPARTMENT:		EXEMPTIONS:

DAY OF WEEK	MORNING		AFTERNOON		OVERTIME		FOR OFFICE USE ONLY	
	IN	OUT	IN	OUT	IN	OUT	REGULAR HOURS	OVERTIME HOURS
MONDAY								
TUESDAY								
WEDNESDAY								
THURSDAY								
FRIDAY								
SATURDAY								
SUNDAY								
TOTAL HOURS								

OVERTIME
AUTHORIZATION_____

EMPLOYEE
SIGNATURE_____

This time sheet must be filled and signed by Employee Daily .
Overtime needs to be authorized by Authority First.

Weekly Time Sheet

EMPLOYEE NAME:	WEEK ENDING:
DEPARTMENT:	EXEMPTIONS:

DAY OF WEEK	MORNING		AFTERNOON		OVERTIME		FOR OFFICE USE ONLY	
	IN	OUT	IN	OUT	IN	OUT	REGULAR HOURS	OVERTIME HOURS
MONDAY								
TUESDAY								
WEDNESDAY								
THURSDAY								
FRIDAY								
SATURDAY								
SUNDAY								
TOTAL HOURS								

OVERTIME
AUTHORIZATION_____

EMPLOYEE
SIGNATURE_____

This time sheet must be filled and signed by Employee Daily .
Overtime needs to be authorized by Authority First.

Weekly Time Sheet

EMPLOYEE NAME:	WEEK ENDING:
DEPARTMENT:	EXEMPTIONS:

DAY OF WEEK	MORNING		AFTERNOON		OVERTIME		FOR OFFICE USE ONLY	
	IN	OUT	IN	OUT	IN	OUT	REGULAR HOURS	OVERTIME HOURS
MONDAY								
TUESDAY								
WEDNESDAY								
THURSDAY								
FRIDAY								
SATURDAY								
SUNDAY								
TOTAL HOURS								

OVERTIME
AUTHORIZATION_____

EMPLOYEE
SIGNATURE_____

This time sheet must be filled and signed by Employee Daily .
Overtime needs to be authorized by Authority First.

Weekly Time Sheet

EMPLOYEE NAME:	WEEK ENDING:
DEPARTMENT:	EXEMPTIONS:

DAY OF WEEK	MORNING		AFTERNOON		OVERTIME		FOR OFFICE USE ONLY	
	IN	OUT	IN	OUT	IN	OUT	REGULAR HOURS	OVERTIME HOURS
MONDAY								
TUESDAY								
WEDNESDAY								
THURSDAY								
FRIDAY								
SATURDAY								
SUNDAY								
TOTAL HOURS								

OVERTIME AUTHORIZATION_____

EMPLOYEE SIGNATURE_____

This time sheet must be filled and signed by Employee Daily .
Overtime needs to be authorized by Authority First.

Weekly Time Sheet

EMPLOYEE NAME:	WEEK ENDING:
DEPARTMENT:	EXEMPTIONS:

DAY OF WEEK	MORNING		AFTERNOON		OVERTIME		FOR OFFICE USE ONLY	
	IN	OUT	IN	OUT	IN	OUT	REGULAR HOURS	OVERTIME HOURS
MONDAY								
TUESDAY								
WEDNESDAY								
THURSDAY								
FRIDAY								
SATURDAY								
SUNDAY								
TOTAL HOURS								

OVERTIME
AUTHORIZATION_____

EMPLOYEE
SIGNATURE_____

This time sheet must be filled and signed by Employee Daily .
Overtime needs to be authorized by Authority First.

Weekly Time Sheet

EMPLOYEE NAME:	WEEK ENDING:
DEPARTMENT:	EXEMPTIONS:

DAY OF WEEK	MORNING		AFTERNOON		OVERTIME		FOR OFFICE USE ONLY	
	IN	OUT	IN	OUT	IN	OUT	REGULAR HOURS	OVERTIME HOURS
MONDAY								
TUESDAY								
WEDNESDAY								
THURSDAY								
FRIDAY								
SATURDAY								
SUNDAY								
TOTAL HOURS								

OVERTIME
AUTHORIZATION_____

EMPLOYEE
SIGNATURE_____

This time sheet must be filled and signed by Employee Daily .
Overtime needs to be authorized by Authority First.

Weekly Time Sheet

EMPLOYEE NAME:		WEEK ENDING:	
DEPARTMENT:		EXEMPTIONS:	

DAY OF WEEK	MORNING		AFTERNOON		OVERTIME		FOR OFFICE USE ONLY	
	IN	OUT	IN	OUT	IN	OUT	REGULAR HOURS	OVERTIME HOURS
MONDAY								
TUESDAY								
WEDNESDAY								
THURSDAY								
FRIDAY								
SATURDAY								
SUNDAY								
TOTAL HOURS								

OVERTIME AUTHORIZATION_____

EMPLOYEE SIGNATURE_____

This time sheet must be filled and signed by Employee Daily .
Overtime needs to be authorized by Authority First.

Weekly Time Sheet

EMPLOYEE NAME:	WEEK ENDING:
DEPARTMENT:	EXEMPTIONS:

DAY OF WEEK	MORNING		AFTERNOON		OVERTIME		FOR OFFICE USE ONLY	
	IN	OUT	IN	OUT	IN	OUT	REGULAR HOURS	OVERTIME HOURS
MONDAY								
TUESDAY								
WEDNESDAY								
THURSDAY								
FRIDAY								
SATURDAY								
SUNDAY								
TOTAL HOURS								

OVERTIME
AUTHORIZATION_____

EMPLOYEE
SIGNATURE_____

This time sheet must be filled and signed by Employee Daily .
Overtime needs to be authorized by Authority First.

Weekly Time Sheet

EMPLOYEE NAME:	WEEK ENDING:
DEPARTMENT:	EXEMPTIONS:

DAY OF WEEK	MORNING		AFTERNOON		OVERTIME		FOR OFFICE USE ONLY	
	IN	OUT	IN	OUT	IN	OUT	REGULAR HOURS	OVERTIME HOURS
MONDAY								
TUESDAY								
WEDNESDAY								
THURSDAY								
FRIDAY								
SATURDAY								
SUNDAY								
TOTAL HOURS								

OVERTIME AUTHORIZATION_____ **EMPLOYEE SIGNATURE**_____

This time sheet must be filled and signed by Employee Daily .
Overtime needs to be authorized by Authority First.

Weekly Time Sheet

EMPLOYEE NAME:	WEEK ENDING:
DEPARTMENT:	EXEMPTIONS:

DAY OF WEEK	MORNING		AFTERNOON		OVERTIME		FOR OFFICE USE ONLY	
	IN	OUT	IN	OUT	IN	OUT	REGULAR HOURS	OVERTIME HOURS
MONDAY								
TUESDAY								
WEDNESDAY								
THURSDAY								
FRIDAY								
SATURDAY								
SUNDAY								
TOTAL HOURS								

OVERTIME
AUTHORIZATION_____

EMPLOYEE
SIGNATURE_____

This time sheet must be filled and signed by Employee Daily .
Overtime needs to be authorized by Authority First.

Weekly Time Sheet

EMPLOYEE NAME:	WEEK ENDING:
DEPARTMENT:	EXEMPTIONS:

DAY OF WEEK	MORNING		AFTERNOON		OVERTIME		FOR OFFICE USE ONLY	
	IN	OUT	IN	OUT	IN	OUT	REGULAR HOURS	OVERTIME HOURS
MONDAY								
TUESDAY								
WEDNESDAY								
THURSDAY								
FRIDAY								
SATURDAY								
SUNDAY								
TOTAL HOURS								

OVERTIME AUTHORIZATION_____   **EMPLOYEE SIGNATURE**_____

This time sheet must be filled and signed by Employee Daily .
Overtime needs to be authorized by Authority First.

Weekly Time Sheet

EMPLOYEE NAME:	WEEK ENDING:
DEPARTMENT:	EXEMPTIONS:

DAY OF WEEK	MORNING		AFTERNOON		OVERTIME		FOR OFFICE USE ONLY	
	IN	OUT	IN	OUT	IN	OUT	REGULAR HOURS	OVERTIME HOURS
MONDAY								
TUESDAY								
WEDNESDAY								
THURSDAY								
FRIDAY								
SATURDAY								
SUNDAY								
TOTAL HOURS								

OVERTIME
AUTHORIZATION_____

EMPLOYEE
SIGNATURE_____

This time sheet must be filled and signed by Employee Daily .
Overtime needs to be authorized by Authority First.

Weekly Time Sheet

EMPLOYEE NAME:	WEEK ENDING:
DEPARTMENT:	EXEMPTIONS:

DAY OF WEEK	MORNING		AFTERNOON		OVERTIME		FOR OFFICE USE ONLY	
	IN	OUT	IN	OUT	IN	OUT	REGULAR HOURS	OVERTIME HOURS
MONDAY								
TUESDAY								
WEDNESDAY								
THURSDAY								
FRIDAY								
SATURDAY								
SUNDAY								
TOTAL HOURS								

OVERTIME AUTHORIZATION_____

EMPLOYEE SIGNATURE_____

This time sheet must be filled and signed by Employee Daily .
Overtime needs to be authorized by Authority First.

Weekly Time Sheet

EMPLOYEE NAME:	WEEK ENDING:
DEPARTMENT:	EXEMPTIONS:

DAY OF WEEK	MORNING		AFTERNOON		OVERTIME		FOR OFFICE USE ONLY	
	IN	OUT	IN	OUT	IN	OUT	REGULAR HOURS	OVERTIME HOURS
MONDAY								
TUESDAY								
WEDNESDAY								
THURSDAY								
FRIDAY								
SATURDAY								
SUNDAY								
TOTAL HOURS								

OVERTIME AUTHORIZATION_____   **EMPLOYEE SIGNATURE**_____

This time sheet must be filled and signed by Employee Daily .
Overtime needs to be authorized by Authority First.

Weekly Time Sheet

EMPLOYEE NAME:	WEEK ENDING:
DEPARTMENT:	EXEMPTIONS:

DAY OF WEEK	MORNING		AFTERNOON		OVERTIME		FOR OFFICE USE ONLY	
	IN	OUT	IN	OUT	IN	OUT	REGULAR HOURS	OVERTIME HOURS
MONDAY								
TUESDAY								
WEDNESDAY								
THURSDAY								
FRIDAY								
SATURDAY								
SUNDAY								
TOTAL HOURS								

OVERTIME AUTHORIZATION_____   **EMPLOYEE SIGNATURE**_____

This time sheet must be filled and signed by Employee Daily .
Overtime needs to be authorized by Authority First.

Weekly Time Sheet

| EMPLOYEE NAME: | | WEEK ENDING: |
| DEPARTMENT: | | EXEMPTIONS: |

DAY OF WEEK	MORNING		AFTERNOON		OVERTIME		FOR OFFICE USE ONLY	
	IN	OUT	IN	OUT	IN	OUT	REGULAR HOURS	OVERTIME HOURS
MONDAY								
TUESDAY								
WEDNESDAY								
THURSDAY								
FRIDAY								
SATURDAY								
SUNDAY								
TOTAL HOURS								

OVERTIME AUTHORIZATION_____   EMPLOYEE SIGNATURE_____

This time sheet must be filled and signed by Employee Daily .
Overtime needs to be authorized by Authority First.

Weekly Time Sheet

EMPLOYEE NAME:	WEEK ENDING:
DEPARTMENT:	EXEMPTIONS:

DAY OF WEEK	MORNING		AFTERNOON		OVERTIME		FOR OFFICE USE ONLY	
	IN	OUT	IN	OUT	IN	OUT	REGULAR HOURS	OVERTIME HOURS
MONDAY								
TUESDAY								
WEDNESDAY								
THURSDAY								
FRIDAY								
SATURDAY								
SUNDAY								
TOTAL HOURS								

OVERTIME AUTHORIZATION_____   **EMPLOYEE SIGNATURE**_____

This time sheet must be filled and signed by Employee Daily .
Overtime needs to be authorized by Authority First.

Weekly Time Sheet

EMPLOYEE NAME:	WEEK ENDING:
DEPARTMENT:	EXEMPTIONS:

DAY OF WEEK	MORNING		AFTERNOON		OVERTIME		FOR OFFICE USE ONLY	
	IN	OUT	IN	OUT	IN	OUT	REGULAR HOURS	OVERTIME HOURS
MONDAY								
TUESDAY								
WEDNESDAY								
THURSDAY								
FRIDAY								
SATURDAY								
SUNDAY								
TOTAL HOURS								

OVERTIME
AUTHORIZATION_____

EMPLOYEE
SIGNATURE_____

This time sheet must be filled and signed by Employee Daily .
Overtime needs to be authorized by Authority First.

Weekly Time Sheet

EMPLOYEE NAME:	WEEK ENDING:
DEPARTMENT:	EXEMPTIONS:

DAY OF WEEK	MORNING		AFTERNOON		OVERTIME		FOR OFFICE USE ONLY	
	IN	OUT	IN	OUT	IN	OUT	REGULAR HOURS	OVERTIME HOURS
MONDAY								
TUESDAY								
WEDNESDAY								
THURSDAY								
FRIDAY								
SATURDAY								
SUNDAY								
TOTAL HOURS								

OVERTIME AUTHORIZATION_____   **EMPLOYEE SIGNATURE**_____

This time sheet must be filled and signed by Employee Daily .
Overtime needs to be authorized by Authority First.

Weekly Time Sheet

EMPLOYEE NAME:	WEEK ENDING:
DEPARTMENT:	EXEMPTIONS:

DAY OF WEEK	MORNING		AFTERNOON		OVERTIME		FOR OFFICE USE ONLY	
	IN	OUT	IN	OUT	IN	OUT	REGULAR HOURS	OVERTIME HOURS
MONDAY								
TUESDAY								
WEDNESDAY								
THURSDAY								
FRIDAY								
SATURDAY								
SUNDAY								
TOTAL HOURS								

OVERTIME
AUTHORIZATION_____

EMPLOYEE
SIGNATURE_____

This time sheet must be filled and signed by Employee Daily .
Overtime needs to be authorized by Authority First.

Weekly Time Sheet

EMPLOYEE NAME:	WEEK ENDING:
DEPARTMENT:	EXEMPTIONS:

DAY OF WEEK	MORNING		AFTERNOON		OVERTIME		FOR OFFICE USE ONLY	
	IN	OUT	IN	OUT	IN	OUT	REGULAR HOURS	OVERTIME HOURS
MONDAY								
TUESDAY								
WEDNESDAY								
THURSDAY								
FRIDAY								
SATURDAY								
SUNDAY								
TOTAL HOURS								

OVERTIME AUTHORIZATION_____ **EMPLOYEE SIGNATURE**_____

This time sheet must be filled and signed by Employee Daily .
Overtime needs to be authorized by Authority First.

Weekly Time Sheet

EMPLOYEE NAME:	WEEK ENDING:
DEPARTMENT:	EXEMPTIONS:

DAY OF WEEK	MORNING		AFTERNOON		OVERTIME		FOR OFFICE USE ONLY	
	IN	OUT	IN	OUT	IN	OUT	REGULAR HOURS	OVERTIME HOURS
MONDAY								
TUESDAY								
WEDNESDAY								
THURSDAY								
FRIDAY								
SATURDAY								
SUNDAY								
TOTAL HOURS								

OVERTIME
AUTHORIZATION_____

EMPLOYEE
SIGNATURE_____

This time sheet must be filled and signed by Employee Daily .
Overtime needs to be authorized by Authority First.

Weekly Time Sheet

EMPLOYEE NAME:		WEEK ENDING:
DEPARTMENT:		EXEMPTIONS:

DAY OF WEEK	MORNING		AFTERNOON		OVERTIME		FOR OFFICE USE ONLY	
	IN	OUT	IN	OUT	IN	OUT	REGULAR HOURS	OVERTIME HOURS
MONDAY								
TUESDAY								
WEDNESDAY								
THURSDAY								
FRIDAY								
SATURDAY								
SUNDAY								
TOTAL HOURS								

OVERTIME
AUTHORIZATION_____

EMPLOYEE
SIGNATURE_____

**This time sheet must be filled and signed by Employee Daily .
Overtime needs to be authorized by Authority First.**

Weekly Time Sheet

| EMPLOYEE NAME: | | WEEK ENDING: |
| DEPARTMENT: | | EXEMPTIONS: |

DAY OF WEEK	MORNING		AFTERNOON		OVERTIME		FOR OFFICE USE ONLY	
	IN	OUT	IN	OUT	IN	OUT	REGULAR HOURS	OVERTIME HOURS
MONDAY								
TUESDAY								
WEDNESDAY								
THURSDAY								
FRIDAY								
SATURDAY								
SUNDAY								
TOTAL HOURS								

OVERTIME
AUTHORIZATION_____

EMPLOYEE
SIGNATURE_____

This time sheet must be filled and signed by Employee Daily .
Overtime needs to be authorized by Authority First.

Weekly Time Sheet

EMPLOYEE NAME:		WEEK ENDING:
DEPARTMENT:		EXEMPTIONS:

DAY OF WEEK	MORNING		AFTERNOON		OVERTIME		FOR OFFICE USE ONLY	
	IN	OUT	IN	OUT	IN	OUT	REGULAR HOURS	OVERTIME HOURS
MONDAY								
TUESDAY								
WEDNESDAY								
THURSDAY								
FRIDAY								
SATURDAY								
SUNDAY								
TOTAL HOURS								

OVERTIME AUTHORIZATION_____

EMPLOYEE SIGNATURE_____

This time sheet must be filled and signed by Employee Daily .
Overtime needs to be authorized by Authority First.

Weekly Time Sheet

EMPLOYEE NAME:		WEEK ENDING:
DEPARTMENT:		EXEMPTIONS:

DAY OF WEEK	MORNING		AFTERNOON		OVERTIME		FOR OFFICE USE ONLY	
	IN	OUT	IN	OUT	IN	OUT	REGULAR HOURS	OVERTIME HOURS
MONDAY								
TUESDAY								
WEDNESDAY								
THURSDAY								
FRIDAY								
SATURDAY								
SUNDAY								
TOTAL HOURS								

OVERTIME
AUTHORIZATION_____

EMPLOYEE
SIGNATURE_____

This time sheet must be filled and signed by Employee Daily .
Overtime needs to be authorized by Authority First.

Weekly Time Sheet

EMPLOYEE NAME:

WEEK ENDING:

DEPARTMENT:

EXEMPTIONS:

DAY OF WEEK	MORNING		AFTERNOON		OVERTIME		FOR OFFICE USE ONLY	
	IN	OUT	IN	OUT	IN	OUT	REGULAR HOURS	OVERTIME HOURS
MONDAY								
TUESDAY								
WEDNESDAY								
THURSDAY								
FRIDAY								
SATURDAY								
SUNDAY								
TOTAL HOURS								

OVERTIME
AUTHORIZATION_____

EMPLOYEE
SIGNATURE_____

**This time sheet must be filled and signed by Employee Daily .
Overtime needs to be authorized by Authority First.**

Weekly Time Sheet

EMPLOYEE NAME:	WEEK ENDING:
DEPARTMENT:	EXEMPTIONS:

DAY OF WEEK	MORNING		AFTERNOON		OVERTIME		FOR OFFICE USE ONLY	
	IN	OUT	IN	OUT	IN	OUT	REGULAR HOURS	OVERTIME HOURS
MONDAY								
TUESDAY								
WEDNESDAY								
THURSDAY								
FRIDAY								
SATURDAY								
SUNDAY								
TOTAL HOURS								

OVERTIME
AUTHORIZATION_____

EMPLOYEE
SIGNATURE_____

**This time sheet must be filled and signed by Employee Daily .
Overtime needs to be authorized by Authority First.**

Weekly Time Sheet

EMPLOYEE NAME:	WEEK ENDING:
DEPARTMENT:	EXEMPTIONS:

DAY OF WEEK	MORNING		AFTERNOON		OVERTIME		FOR OFFICE USE ONLY	
	IN	OUT	IN	OUT	IN	OUT	REGULAR HOURS	OVERTIME HOURS
MONDAY								
TUESDAY								
WEDNESDAY								
THURSDAY								
FRIDAY								
SATURDAY								
SUNDAY								
TOTAL HOURS								

OVERTIME AUTHORIZATION_____

EMPLOYEE SIGNATURE_____

This time sheet must be filled and signed by Employee Daily .
Overtime needs to be authorized by Authority First.

Weekly Time Sheet

EMPLOYEE NAME:	WEEK ENDING:
DEPARTMENT:	EXEMPTIONS:

DAY OF WEEK	MORNING		AFTERNOON		OVERTIME		FOR OFFICE USE ONLY	
	IN	OUT	IN	OUT	IN	OUT	REGULAR HOURS	OVERTIME HOURS
MONDAY								
TUESDAY								
WEDNESDAY								
THURSDAY								
FRIDAY								
SATURDAY								
SUNDAY								
TOTAL HOURS								

OVERTIME
AUTHORIZATION_____

EMPLOYEE
SIGNATURE_____

This time sheet must be filled and signed by Employee Daily .
Overtime needs to be authorized by Authority First.

Weekly Time Sheet

EMPLOYEE NAME:		WEEK ENDING:
DEPARTMENT:		EXEMPTIONS:

DAY OF WEEK	MORNING		AFTERNOON		OVERTIME		FOR OFFICE USE ONLY	
	IN	OUT	IN	OUT	IN	OUT	REGULAR HOURS	OVERTIME HOURS
MONDAY								
TUESDAY								
WEDNESDAY								
THURSDAY								
FRIDAY								
SATURDAY								
SUNDAY								
TOTAL HOURS								

OVERTIME AUTHORIZATION_____   EMPLOYEE SIGNATURE_____

This time sheet must be filled and signed by Employee Daily .
Overtime needs to be authorized by Authority First.

Weekly Time Sheet

EMPLOYEE NAME:		WEEK ENDING:
DEPARTMENT:		EXEMPTIONS:

DAY OF WEEK	MORNING		AFTERNOON		OVERTIME		FOR OFFICE USE ONLY	
	IN	OUT	IN	OUT	IN	OUT	REGULAR HOURS	OVERTIME HOURS
MONDAY								
TUESDAY								
WEDNESDAY								
THURSDAY								
FRIDAY								
SATURDAY								
SUNDAY								
TOTAL HOURS								

OVERTIME
AUTHORIZATION_____

EMPLOYEE
SIGNATURE_____

This time sheet must be filled and signed by Employee Daily .
Overtime needs to be authorized by Authority First.

Weekly Time Sheet

EMPLOYEE NAME:	WEEK ENDING:
DEPARTMENT:	EXEMPTIONS:

DAY OF WEEK	MORNING		AFTERNOON		OVERTIME		FOR OFFICE USE ONLY	
	IN	OUT	IN	OUT	IN	OUT	REGULAR HOURS	OVERTIME HOURS
MONDAY								
TUESDAY								
WEDNESDAY								
THURSDAY								
FRIDAY								
SATURDAY								
SUNDAY								
TOTAL HOURS								

OVERTIME AUTHORIZATION_____   **EMPLOYEE SIGNATURE**_____

This time sheet must be filled and signed by Employee Daily .
Overtime needs to be authorized by Authority First.

Weekly Time Sheet

EMPLOYEE NAME:		WEEK ENDING:
DEPARTMENT:		EXEMPTIONS:

DAY OF WEEK	MORNING		AFTERNOON		OVERTIME		FOR OFFICE USE ONLY	
	IN	OUT	IN	OUT	IN	OUT	REGULAR HOURS	OVERTIME HOURS
MONDAY								
TUESDAY								
WEDNESDAY								
THURSDAY								
FRIDAY								
SATURDAY								
SUNDAY								
TOTAL HOURS								

OVERTIME AUTHORIZATION_____ **EMPLOYEE SIGNATURE**_____

This time sheet must be filled and signed by Employee Daily .
Overtime needs to be authorized by Authority First.

Weekly Time Sheet

EMPLOYEE NAME:		WEEK ENDING:
DEPARTMENT:		EXEMPTIONS:

DAY OF WEEK	MORNING		AFTERNOON		OVERTIME		FOR OFFICE USE ONLY	
	IN	OUT	IN	OUT	IN	OUT	REGULAR HOURS	OVERTIME HOURS
MONDAY								
TUESDAY								
WEDNESDAY								
THURSDAY								
FRIDAY								
SATURDAY								
SUNDAY								
TOTAL HOURS								

OVERTIME AUTHORIZATION_____   **EMPLOYEE SIGNATURE**_____

This time sheet must be filled and signed by Employee Daily .
Overtime needs to be authorized by Authority First.

Weekly Time Sheet

EMPLOYEE NAME:	WEEK ENDING:
DEPARTMENT:	EXEMPTIONS:

DAY OF WEEK	MORNING		AFTERNOON		OVERTIME		FOR OFFICE USE ONLY	
	IN	OUT	IN	OUT	IN	OUT	REGULAR HOURS	OVERTIME HOURS
MONDAY								
TUESDAY								
WEDNESDAY								
THURSDAY								
FRIDAY								
SATURDAY								
SUNDAY								
TOTAL HOURS								

OVERTIME
AUTHORIZATION_____

EMPLOYEE
SIGNATURE_____

This time sheet must be filled and signed by Employee Daily .
Overtime needs to be authorized by Authority First.

Weekly Time Sheet

EMPLOYEE NAME:		WEEK ENDING:
DEPARTMENT:		EXEMPTIONS:

DAY OF WEEK	MORNING		AFTERNOON		OVERTIME		FOR OFFICE USE ONLY	
	IN	OUT	IN	OUT	IN	OUT	REGULAR HOURS	OVERTIME HOURS
MONDAY								
TUESDAY								
WEDNESDAY								
THURSDAY								
FRIDAY								
SATURDAY								
SUNDAY								
TOTAL HOURS								

OVERTIME
AUTHORIZATION_____

EMPLOYEE
SIGNATURE_____

This time sheet must be filled and signed by Employee Daily .
Overtime needs to be authorized by Authority First.

Weekly Time Sheet

EMPLOYEE NAME:	WEEK ENDING:
DEPARTMENT:	EXEMPTIONS:

DAY OF WEEK	MORNING		AFTERNOON		OVERTIME		FOR OFFICE USE ONLY	
	IN	OUT	IN	OUT	IN	OUT	REGULAR HOURS	OVERTIME HOURS
MONDAY								
TUESDAY								
WEDNESDAY								
THURSDAY								
FRIDAY								
SATURDAY								
SUNDAY								
TOTAL HOURS								

OVERTIME
AUTHORIZATION_____

EMPLOYEE
SIGNATURE_____

**This time sheet must be filled and signed by Employee Daily .
Overtime needs to be authorized by Authority First.**

Weekly Time Sheet

EMPLOYEE NAME:	WEEK ENDING:
DEPARTMENT:	EXEMPTIONS:

DAY OF WEEK	MORNING		AFTERNOON		OVERTIME		FOR OFFICE USE ONLY	
	IN	OUT	IN	OUT	IN	OUT	REGULAR HOURS	OVERTIME HOURS
MONDAY								
TUESDAY								
WEDNESDAY								
THURSDAY								
FRIDAY								
SATURDAY								
SUNDAY								
TOTAL HOURS								

OVERTIME
AUTHORIZATION_____   EMPLOYEE
SIGNATURE_____

This time sheet must be filled and signed by Employee Daily .
Overtime needs to be authorized by Authority First.

Weekly Time Sheet

EMPLOYEE NAME:	WEEK ENDING:
DEPARTMENT:	EXEMPTIONS:

DAY OF WEEK	MORNING		AFTERNOON		OVERTIME		FOR OFFICE USE ONLY	
	IN	OUT	IN	OUT	IN	OUT	REGULAR HOURS	OVERTIME HOURS
MONDAY								
TUESDAY								
WEDNESDAY								
THURSDAY								
FRIDAY								
SATURDAY								
SUNDAY								
TOTAL HOURS								

OVERTIME
AUTHORIZATION_____

EMPLOYEE
SIGNATURE_____

This time sheet must be filled and signed by Employee Daily .
Overtime needs to be authorized by Authority First.

Weekly Time Sheet

EMPLOYEE NAME:	WEEK ENDING:
DEPARTMENT:	EXEMPTIONS:

DAY OF WEEK	MORNING		AFTERNOON		OVERTIME		FOR OFFICE USE ONLY	
	IN	OUT	IN	OUT	IN	OUT	REGULAR HOURS	OVERTIME HOURS
MONDAY								
TUESDAY								
WEDNESDAY								
THURSDAY								
FRIDAY								
SATURDAY								
SUNDAY								
TOTAL HOURS								

OVERTIME AUTHORIZATION_____   **EMPLOYEE SIGNATURE**_____

This time sheet must be filled and signed by Employee Daily .
Overtime needs to be authorized by Authority First.

Weekly Time Sheet

EMPLOYEE NAME:		WEEK ENDING:	
DEPARTMENT:		EXEMPTIONS:	

DAY OF WEEK	MORNING		AFTERNOON		OVERTIME		FOR OFFICE USE ONLY	
	IN	OUT	IN	OUT	IN	OUT	REGULAR HOURS	OVERTIME HOURS
MONDAY								
TUESDAY								
WEDNESDAY								
THURSDAY								
FRIDAY								
SATURDAY								
SUNDAY								
TOTAL HOURS								

OVERTIME
AUTHORIZATION_____

EMPLOYEE
SIGNATURE_____

This time sheet must be filled and signed by Employee Daily .
Overtime needs to be authorized by Authority First.

Weekly Time Sheet

EMPLOYEE NAME:	WEEK ENDING:
DEPARTMENT:	EXEMPTIONS:

DAY OF WEEK	MORNING		AFTERNOON		OVERTIME		FOR OFFICE USE ONLY	
	IN	OUT	IN	OUT	IN	OUT	REGULAR HOURS	OVERTIME HOURS
MONDAY								
TUESDAY								
WEDNESDAY								
THURSDAY								
FRIDAY								
SATURDAY								
SUNDAY								
TOTAL HOURS								

OVERTIME AUTHORIZATION_____   **EMPLOYEE SIGNATURE**_____

This time sheet must be filled and signed by Employee Daily .
Overtime needs to be authorized by Authority First.

Weekly Time Sheet

EMPLOYEE NAME:	WEEK ENDING:
DEPARTMENT:	EXEMPTIONS:

DAY OF WEEK	MORNING		AFTERNOON		OVERTIME		FOR OFFICE USE ONLY	
	IN	OUT	IN	OUT	IN	OUT	REGULAR HOURS	OVERTIME HOURS
MONDAY								
TUESDAY								
WEDNESDAY								
THURSDAY								
FRIDAY								
SATURDAY								
SUNDAY								
TOTAL HOURS								

OVERTIME AUTHORIZATION_____

EMPLOYEE SIGNATURE_____

This time sheet must be filled and signed by Employee Daily .
Overtime needs to be authorized by Authority First.

Weekly Time Sheet

EMPLOYEE NAME:		WEEK ENDING:
DEPARTMENT:		EXEMPTIONS:

DAY OF WEEK	MORNING		AFTERNOON		OVERTIME		FOR OFFICE USE ONLY	
	IN	OUT	IN	OUT	IN	OUT	REGULAR HOURS	OVERTIME HOURS
MONDAY								
TUESDAY								
WEDNESDAY								
THURSDAY								
FRIDAY								
SATURDAY								
SUNDAY								
TOTAL HOURS								

OVERTIME AUTHORIZATION_____

EMPLOYEE SIGNATURE_____

This time sheet must be filled and signed by Employee Daily .
Overtime needs to be authorized by Authority First.

Weekly Time Sheet

EMPLOYEE NAME:	WEEK ENDING:
DEPARTMENT:	EXEMPTIONS:

DAY OF WEEK	MORNING		AFTERNOON		OVERTIME		FOR OFFICE USE ONLY	
	IN	OUT	IN	OUT	IN	OUT	REGULAR HOURS	OVERTIME HOURS
MONDAY								
TUESDAY								
WEDNESDAY								
THURSDAY								
FRIDAY								
SATURDAY								
SUNDAY								
TOTAL HOURS								

OVERTIME
AUTHORIZATION_____   EMPLOYEE
SIGNATURE_____

This time sheet must be filled and signed by Employee Daily .
Overtime needs to be authorized by Authority First.

Weekly Time Sheet

EMPLOYEE NAME:	WEEK ENDING:
DEPARTMENT:	EXEMPTIONS:

DAY OF WEEK	MORNING		AFTERNOON		OVERTIME		FOR OFFICE USE ONLY	
	IN	OUT	IN	OUT	IN	OUT	REGULAR HOURS	OVERTIME HOURS
MONDAY								
TUESDAY								
WEDNESDAY								
THURSDAY								
FRIDAY								
SATURDAY								
SUNDAY								
TOTAL HOURS								

OVERTIME AUTHORIZATION_____   **EMPLOYEE SIGNATURE**_____

This time sheet must be filled and signed by Employee Daily .
Overtime needs to be authorized by Authority First.

Weekly Time Sheet

EMPLOYEE NAME:	WEEK ENDING:
DEPARTMENT:	EXEMPTIONS:

DAY OF WEEK	MORNING		AFTERNOON		OVERTIME		FOR OFFICE USE ONLY	
	IN	OUT	IN	OUT	IN	OUT	REGULAR HOURS	OVERTIME HOURS
MONDAY								
TUESDAY								
WEDNESDAY								
THURSDAY								
FRIDAY								
SATURDAY								
SUNDAY								
TOTAL HOURS								

OVERTIME
AUTHORIZATION_____

EMPLOYEE
SIGNATURE_____

**This time sheet must be filled and signed by Employee Daily .
Overtime needs to be authorized by Authority First.**

Weekly Time Sheet

EMPLOYEE NAME:	WEEK ENDING:
DEPARTMENT:	EXEMPTIONS:

DAY OF WEEK	MORNING		AFTERNOON		OVERTIME		FOR OFFICE USE ONLY	
	IN	OUT	IN	OUT	IN	OUT	REGULAR HOURS	OVERTIME HOURS
MONDAY								
TUESDAY								
WEDNESDAY								
THURSDAY								
FRIDAY								
SATURDAY								
SUNDAY								
TOTAL HOURS								

OVERTIME AUTHORIZATION_____ **EMPLOYEE SIGNATURE**_____

This time sheet must be filled and signed by Employee Daily .
Overtime needs to be authorized by Authority First.

Weekly Time Sheet

EMPLOYEE NAME:	WEEK ENDING:
DEPARTMENT:	EXEMPTIONS:

DAY OF WEEK	MORNING		AFTERNOON		OVERTIME		FOR OFFICE USE ONLY	
	IN	OUT	IN	OUT	IN	OUT	REGULAR HOURS	OVERTIME HOURS
MONDAY								
TUESDAY								
WEDNESDAY								
THURSDAY								
FRIDAY								
SATURDAY								
SUNDAY								
TOTAL HOURS								

OVERTIME
AUTHORIZATION_____

EMPLOYEE
SIGNATURE_____

This time sheet must be filled and signed by Employee Daily .
Overtime needs to be authorized by Authority First.

Weekly Time Sheet

EMPLOYEE NAME:	WEEK ENDING:
DEPARTMENT:	EXEMPTIONS:

DAY OF WEEK	MORNING		AFTERNOON		OVERTIME		FOR OFFICE USE ONLY	
	IN	OUT	IN	OUT	IN	OUT	REGULAR HOURS	OVERTIME HOURS
MONDAY								
TUESDAY								
WEDNESDAY								
THURSDAY								
FRIDAY								
SATURDAY								
SUNDAY								
TOTAL HOURS								

OVERTIME
AUTHORIZATION_____

EMPLOYEE
SIGNATURE_____

This time sheet must be filled and signed by Employee Daily .
Overtime needs to be authorized by Authority First.

Weekly Time Sheet

EMPLOYEE NAME:		WEEK ENDING:
DEPARTMENT:		EXEMPTIONS:

DAY OF WEEK	MORNING		AFTERNOON		OVERTIME		FOR OFFICE USE ONLY	
	IN	OUT	IN	OUT	IN	OUT	REGULAR HOURS	OVERTIME HOURS
MONDAY								
TUESDAY								
WEDNESDAY								
THURSDAY								
FRIDAY								
SATURDAY								
SUNDAY								
TOTAL HOURS								

OVERTIME
AUTHORIZATION_____

EMPLOYEE
SIGNATURE_____

**This time sheet must be filled and signed by Employee Daily .
Overtime needs to be authorized by Authority First.**

Weekly Time Sheet

EMPLOYEE NAME:		WEEK ENDING:
DEPARTMENT:		EXEMPTIONS:

DAY OF WEEK	MORNING		AFTERNOON		OVERTIME		FOR OFFICE USE ONLY	
	IN	OUT	IN	OUT	IN	OUT	REGULAR HOURS	OVERTIME HOURS
MONDAY								
TUESDAY								
WEDNESDAY								
THURSDAY								
FRIDAY								
SATURDAY								
SUNDAY								
TOTAL HOURS								

OVERTIME AUTHORIZATION_____   **EMPLOYEE SIGNATURE**_____

This time sheet must be filled and signed by Employee Daily .
Overtime needs to be authorized by Authority First.

Weekly Time Sheet

EMPLOYEE NAME:	WEEK ENDING:
DEPARTMENT:	EXEMPTIONS:

DAY OF WEEK	MORNING		AFTERNOON		OVERTIME		FOR OFFICE USE ONLY	
	IN	OUT	IN	OUT	IN	OUT	REGULAR HOURS	OVERTIME HOURS
MONDAY								
TUESDAY								
WEDNESDAY								
THURSDAY								
FRIDAY								
SATURDAY								
SUNDAY								
TOTAL HOURS								

OVERTIME
AUTHORIZATION_____

EMPLOYEE
SIGNATURE_____

This time sheet must be filled and signed by Employee Daily .
Overtime needs to be authorized by Authority First.

Weekly Time Sheet

| EMPLOYEE NAME: | | WEEK ENDING: |
| DEPARTMENT: | | EXEMPTIONS: |

DAY OF WEEK	MORNING		AFTERNOON		OVERTIME		FOR OFFICE USE ONLY	
	IN	OUT	IN	OUT	IN	OUT	REGULAR HOURS	OVERTIME HOURS
MONDAY								
TUESDAY								
WEDNESDAY								
THURSDAY								
FRIDAY								
SATURDAY								
SUNDAY								
TOTAL HOURS								

OVERTIME
AUTHORIZATION_____

EMPLOYEE
SIGNATURE_____

This time sheet must be filled and signed by Employee Daily .
Overtime needs to be authorized by Authority First.

Weekly Time Sheet

EMPLOYEE NAME:	WEEK ENDING:
DEPARTMENT:	EXEMPTIONS:

DAY OF WEEK	MORNING		AFTERNOON		OVERTIME		FOR OFFICE USE ONLY	
	IN	OUT	IN	OUT	IN	OUT	REGULAR HOURS	OVERTIME HOURS
MONDAY								
TUESDAY								
WEDNESDAY								
THURSDAY								
FRIDAY								
SATURDAY								
SUNDAY								
TOTAL HOURS								

OVERTIME
AUTHORIZATION_____

EMPLOYEE
SIGNATURE_____

This time sheet must be filled and signed by Employee Daily .
Overtime needs to be authorized by Authority First.

Weekly Time Sheet

EMPLOYEE NAME:		WEEK ENDING:
DEPARTMENT:		EXEMPTIONS:

DAY OF WEEK	MORNING		AFTERNOON		OVERTIME		FOR OFFICE USE ONLY	
	IN	OUT	IN	OUT	IN	OUT	REGULAR HOURS	OVERTIME HOURS
MONDAY								
TUESDAY								
WEDNESDAY								
THURSDAY								
FRIDAY								
SATURDAY								
SUNDAY								
TOTAL HOURS								

OVERTIME AUTHORIZATION_____   **EMPLOYEE SIGNATURE**_____

This time sheet must be filled and signed by Employee Daily .
Overtime needs to be authorized by Authority First.

Weekly Time Sheet

EMPLOYEE NAME:	WEEK ENDING:
DEPARTMENT:	EXEMPTIONS:

DAY OF WEEK	MORNING		AFTERNOON		OVERTIME		FOR OFFICE USE ONLY	
	IN	OUT	IN	OUT	IN	OUT	REGULAR HOURS	OVERTIME HOURS
MONDAY								
TUESDAY								
WEDNESDAY								
THURSDAY								
FRIDAY								
SATURDAY								
SUNDAY								
TOTAL HOURS								

OVERTIME
AUTHORIZATION_____

EMPLOYEE
SIGNATURE_____

This time sheet must be filled and signed by Employee Daily .
Overtime needs to be authorized by Authority First.

Weekly Time Sheet

| EMPLOYEE NAME: | | WEEK ENDING: |
| DEPARTMENT: | | EXEMPTIONS: |

DAY OF WEEK	MORNING		AFTERNOON		OVERTIME		FOR OFFICE USE ONLY	
	IN	OUT	IN	OUT	IN	OUT	REGULAR HOURS	OVERTIME HOURS
MONDAY								
TUESDAY								
WEDNESDAY								
THURSDAY								
FRIDAY								
SATURDAY								
SUNDAY								
TOTAL HOURS								

OVERTIME AUTHORIZATION_____   EMPLOYEE SIGNATURE_____

This time sheet must be filled and signed by Employee Daily .
Overtime needs to be authorized by Authority First.

Weekly Time Sheet

EMPLOYEE NAME:		WEEK ENDING:
DEPARTMENT:		EXEMPTIONS:

DAY OF WEEK	MORNING		AFTERNOON		OVERTIME		FOR OFFICE USE ONLY	
	IN	OUT	IN	OUT	IN	OUT	REGULAR HOURS	OVERTIME HOURS
MONDAY								
TUESDAY								
WEDNESDAY								
THURSDAY								
FRIDAY								
SATURDAY								
SUNDAY								
TOTAL HOURS								

OVERTIME
AUTHORIZATION_____

EMPLOYEE
SIGNATURE_____

This time sheet must be filled and signed by Employee Daily .
Overtime needs to be authorized by Authority First.

Weekly Time Sheet

EMPLOYEE NAME:	WEEK ENDING:
DEPARTMENT:	EXEMPTIONS:

DAY OF WEEK	MORNING		AFTERNOON		OVERTIME		FOR OFFICE USE ONLY	
	IN	OUT	IN	OUT	IN	OUT	REGULAR HOURS	OVERTIME HOURS
MONDAY								
TUESDAY								
WEDNESDAY								
THURSDAY								
FRIDAY								
SATURDAY								
SUNDAY								
TOTAL HOURS								

OVERTIME AUTHORIZATION_____

EMPLOYEE SIGNATURE_____

**This time sheet must be filled and signed by Employee Daily .
Overtime needs to be authorized by Authority First.**

Weekly Time Sheet

EMPLOYEE NAME:	WEEK ENDING:
DEPARTMENT:	EXEMPTIONS:

DAY OF WEEK	MORNING		AFTERNOON		OVERTIME		FOR OFFICE USE ONLY	
	IN	OUT	IN	OUT	IN	OUT	REGULAR HOURS	OVERTIME HOURS
MONDAY								
TUESDAY								
WEDNESDAY								
THURSDAY								
FRIDAY								
SATURDAY								
SUNDAY								
TOTAL HOURS								

OVERTIME
AUTHORIZATION_____

EMPLOYEE
SIGNATURE_____

This time sheet must be filled and signed by Employee Daily .
Overtime needs to be authorized by Authority First.

Weekly Time Sheet

| EMPLOYEE NAME: | | WEEK ENDING: |
| DEPARTMENT: | | EXEMPTIONS: |

DAY OF WEEK	MORNING		AFTERNOON		OVERTIME		FOR OFFICE USE ONLY	
	IN	OUT	IN	OUT	IN	OUT	REGULAR HOURS	OVERTIME HOURS
MONDAY								
TUESDAY								
WEDNESDAY								
THURSDAY								
FRIDAY								
SATURDAY								
SUNDAY								
TOTAL HOURS								

OVERTIME
AUTHORIZATION_____

EMPLOYEE
SIGNATURE_____

This time sheet must be filled and signed by Employee Daily .
Overtime needs to be authorized by Authority First.

Weekly Time Sheet

EMPLOYEE NAME:	WEEK ENDING:
DEPARTMENT:	EXEMPTIONS:

DAY OF WEEK	MORNING		AFTERNOON		OVERTIME		FOR OFFICE USE ONLY	
	IN	OUT	IN	OUT	IN	OUT	REGULAR HOURS	OVERTIME HOURS
MONDAY								
TUESDAY								
WEDNESDAY								
THURSDAY								
FRIDAY								
SATURDAY								
SUNDAY								
TOTAL HOURS								

OVERTIME
AUTHORIZATION_____

EMPLOYEE
SIGNATURE_____

This time sheet must be filled and signed by Employee Daily .
Overtime needs to be authorized by Authority First.

Weekly Time Sheet

EMPLOYEE NAME:	WEEK ENDING:
DEPARTMENT:	EXEMPTIONS:

DAY OF WEEK	MORNING		AFTERNOON		OVERTIME		FOR OFFICE USE ONLY	
	IN	OUT	IN	OUT	IN	OUT	REGULAR HOURS	OVERTIME HOURS
MONDAY								
TUESDAY								
WEDNESDAY								
THURSDAY								
FRIDAY								
SATURDAY								
SUNDAY								
TOTAL HOURS								

OVERTIME
AUTHORIZATION_____

EMPLOYEE
SIGNATURE_____

This time sheet must be filled and signed by Employee Daily .
Overtime needs to be authorized by Authority First.

Weekly Time Sheet

EMPLOYEE NAME:	WEEK ENDING:
DEPARTMENT:	EXEMPTIONS:

DAY OF WEEK	MORNING		AFTERNOON		OVERTIME		FOR OFFICE USE ONLY	
	IN	OUT	IN	OUT	IN	OUT	REGULAR HOURS	OVERTIME HOURS
MONDAY								
TUESDAY								
WEDNESDAY								
THURSDAY								
FRIDAY								
SATURDAY								
SUNDAY								
TOTAL HOURS								

OVERTIME AUTHORIZATION_____ **EMPLOYEE SIGNATURE**_____

This time sheet must be filled and signed by Employee Daily .
Overtime needs to be authorized by Authority First.

Weekly Time Sheet

EMPLOYEE NAME:		WEEK ENDING:
DEPARTMENT:		EXEMPTIONS:

DAY OF WEEK	MORNING		AFTERNOON		OVERTIME		FOR OFFICE USE ONLY	
	IN	OUT	IN	OUT	IN	OUT	REGULAR HOURS	OVERTIME HOURS
MONDAY								
TUESDAY								
WEDNESDAY								
THURSDAY								
FRIDAY								
SATURDAY								
SUNDAY								
TOTAL HOURS								

OVERTIME
AUTHORIZATION_____

EMPLOYEE
SIGNATURE_____

**This time sheet must be filled and signed by Employee Daily .
Overtime needs to be authorized by Authority First.**

Weekly Time Sheet

EMPLOYEE NAME:		WEEK ENDING:	
DEPARTMENT:		EXEMPTIONS:	

DAY OF WEEK	MORNING		AFTERNOON		OVERTIME		FOR OFFICE USE ONLY	
	IN	OUT	IN	OUT	IN	OUT	REGULAR HOURS	OVERTIME HOURS
MONDAY								
TUESDAY								
WEDNESDAY								
THURSDAY								
FRIDAY								
SATURDAY								
SUNDAY								
TOTAL HOURS								

OVERTIME
AUTHORIZATION_____

EMPLOYEE
SIGNATURE_____

This time sheet must be filled and signed by Employee Daily .
Overtime needs to be authorized by Authority First.

Weekly Time Sheet

EMPLOYEE NAME:		WEEK ENDING:
DEPARTMENT:		EXEMPTIONS:

DAY OF WEEK	MORNING		AFTERNOON		OVERTIME		FOR OFFICE USE ONLY	
	IN	OUT	IN	OUT	IN	OUT	REGULAR HOURS	OVERTIME HOURS
MONDAY								
TUESDAY								
WEDNESDAY								
THURSDAY								
FRIDAY								
SATURDAY								
SUNDAY								
TOTAL HOURS								

OVERTIME AUTHORIZATION_____   **EMPLOYEE SIGNATURE**_____

**This time sheet must be filled and signed by Employee Daily .
Overtime needs to be authorized by Authority First.**

Weekly Time Sheet

EMPLOYEE NAME:	WEEK ENDING:
DEPARTMENT:	EXEMPTIONS:

DAY OF WEEK	MORNING		AFTERNOON		OVERTIME		FOR OFFICE USE ONLY	
	IN	OUT	IN	OUT	IN	OUT	REGULAR HOURS	OVERTIME HOURS
MONDAY								
TUESDAY								
WEDNESDAY								
THURSDAY								
FRIDAY								
SATURDAY								
SUNDAY								
TOTAL HOURS								

OVERTIME
AUTHORIZATION_____

EMPLOYEE
SIGNATURE_____

**This time sheet must be filled and signed by Employee Daily .
Overtime needs to be authorized by Authority First.**

Weekly Time Sheet

EMPLOYEE NAME:	WEEK ENDING:
DEPARTMENT:	EXEMPTIONS:

DAY OF WEEK	MORNING		AFTERNOON		OVERTIME		FOR OFFICE USE ONLY	
	IN	OUT	IN	OUT	IN	OUT	REGULAR HOURS	OVERTIME HOURS
MONDAY								
TUESDAY								
WEDNESDAY								
THURSDAY								
FRIDAY								
SATURDAY								
SUNDAY								
TOTAL HOURS								

OVERTIME AUTHORIZATION_____   **EMPLOYEE SIGNATURE**_____

This time sheet must be filled and signed by Employee Daily .
Overtime needs to be authorized by Authority First.

Weekly Time Sheet

EMPLOYEE NAME:		WEEK ENDING:
DEPARTMENT:		EXEMPTIONS:

DAY OF WEEK	MORNING		AFTERNOON		OVERTIME		FOR OFFICE USE ONLY	
	IN	OUT	IN	OUT	IN	OUT	REGULAR HOURS	OVERTIME HOURS
MONDAY								
TUESDAY								
WEDNESDAY								
THURSDAY								
FRIDAY								
SATURDAY								
SUNDAY								
TOTAL HOURS								

OVERTIME
AUTHORIZATION_____

EMPLOYEE
SIGNATURE_____

This time sheet must be filled and signed by Employee Daily .
Overtime needs to be authorized by Authority First.

Weekly Time Sheet

EMPLOYEE NAME:		WEEK ENDING:
DEPARTMENT:		EXEMPTIONS:

DAY OF WEEK	MORNING		AFTERNOON		OVERTIME		FOR OFFICE USE ONLY	
	IN	OUT	IN	OUT	IN	OUT	REGULAR HOURS	OVERTIME HOURS
MONDAY								
TUESDAY								
WEDNESDAY								
THURSDAY								
FRIDAY								
SATURDAY								
SUNDAY								
TOTAL HOURS								

OVERTIME
AUTHORIZATION_____

EMPLOYEE
SIGNATURE_____

This time sheet must be filled and signed by Employee Daily .
Overtime needs to be authorized by Authority First.

Weekly Time Sheet

EMPLOYEE NAME:		WEEK ENDING:
DEPARTMENT:		EXEMPTIONS:

DAY OF WEEK	MORNING		AFTERNOON		OVERTIME		FOR OFFICE USE ONLY	
	IN	OUT	IN	OUT	IN	OUT	REGULAR HOURS	OVERTIME HOURS
MONDAY								
TUESDAY								
WEDNESDAY								
THURSDAY								
FRIDAY								
SATURDAY								
SUNDAY								
TOTAL HOURS								

OVERTIME
AUTHORIZATION_____

EMPLOYEE
SIGNATURE_____

This time sheet must be filled and signed by Employee Daily .
Overtime needs to be authorized by Authority First.

Weekly Time Sheet

EMPLOYEE NAME:		WEEK ENDING:	
DEPARTMENT:		EXEMPTIONS:	

DAY OF WEEK	MORNING		AFTERNOON		OVERTIME		FOR OFFICE USE ONLY	
	IN	OUT	IN	OUT	IN	OUT	REGULAR HOURS	OVERTIME HOURS
MONDAY								
TUESDAY								
WEDNESDAY								
THURSDAY								
FRIDAY								
SATURDAY								
SUNDAY								
TOTAL HOURS								

OVERTIME
AUTHORIZATION_____

EMPLOYEE
SIGNATURE_____

This time sheet must be filled and signed by Employee Daily .
Overtime needs to be authorized by Authority First.

Weekly Time Sheet

EMPLOYEE NAME:	WEEK ENDING:
DEPARTMENT:	EXEMPTIONS:

DAY OF WEEK	MORNING		AFTERNOON		OVERTIME		FOR OFFICE USE ONLY	
	IN	OUT	IN	OUT	IN	OUT	REGULAR HOURS	OVERTIME HOURS
MONDAY								
TUESDAY								
WEDNESDAY								
THURSDAY								
FRIDAY								
SATURDAY								
SUNDAY								
TOTAL HOURS								

OVERTIME
AUTHORIZATION_____

EMPLOYEE
SIGNATURE_____

This time sheet must be filled and signed by Employee Daily .
Overtime needs to be authorized by Authority First.

Weekly Time Sheet

EMPLOYEE NAME:	WEEK ENDING:
DEPARTMENT:	EXEMPTIONS:

DAY OF WEEK	MORNING		AFTERNOON		OVERTIME		FOR OFFICE USE ONLY	
	IN	OUT	IN	OUT	IN	OUT	REGULAR HOURS	OVERTIME HOURS
MONDAY								
TUESDAY								
WEDNESDAY								
THURSDAY								
FRIDAY								
SATURDAY								
SUNDAY								
TOTAL HOURS								

OVERTIME
AUTHORIZATION_____

EMPLOYEE
SIGNATURE_____

This time sheet must be filled and signed by Employee Daily .
Overtime needs to be authorized by Authority First.

Weekly Time Sheet

EMPLOYEE NAME:	WEEK ENDING:
DEPARTMENT:	EXEMPTIONS:

DAY OF WEEK	MORNING		AFTERNOON		OVERTIME		FOR OFFICE USE ONLY	
	IN	OUT	IN	OUT	IN	OUT	REGULAR HOURS	OVERTIME HOURS
MONDAY								
TUESDAY								
WEDNESDAY								
THURSDAY								
FRIDAY								
SATURDAY								
SUNDAY								
TOTAL HOURS								

OVERTIME
AUTHORIZATION_____

EMPLOYEE
SIGNATURE_____

This time sheet must be filled and signed by Employee Daily .
Overtime needs to be authorized by Authority First.

Weekly Time Sheet

EMPLOYEE NAME:	WEEK ENDING:
DEPARTMENT:	EXEMPTIONS:

DAY OF WEEK	MORNING		AFTERNOON		OVERTIME		FOR OFFICE USE ONLY	
	IN	OUT	IN	OUT	IN	OUT	REGULAR HOURS	OVERTIME HOURS
MONDAY								
TUESDAY								
WEDNESDAY								
THURSDAY								
FRIDAY								
SATURDAY								
SUNDAY								
TOTAL HOURS								

OVERTIME AUTHORIZATION_____   **EMPLOYEE SIGNATURE**_____

This time sheet must be filled and signed by Employee Daily .
Overtime needs to be authorized by Authority First.

Weekly Time Sheet

EMPLOYEE NAME:	WEEK ENDING:
DEPARTMENT:	EXEMPTIONS:

DAY OF WEEK	MORNING		AFTERNOON		OVERTIME		FOR OFFICE USE ONLY	
	IN	OUT	IN	OUT	IN	OUT	REGULAR HOURS	OVERTIME HOURS
MONDAY								
TUESDAY								
WEDNESDAY								
THURSDAY								
FRIDAY								
SATURDAY								
SUNDAY								
TOTAL HOURS								

OVERTIME
AUTHORIZATION_____

EMPLOYEE
SIGNATURE_____

This time sheet must be filled and signed by Employee Daily .
Overtime needs to be authorized by Authority First.

Weekly Time Sheet

EMPLOYEE NAME:	WEEK ENDING:
DEPARTMENT:	EXEMPTIONS:

DAY OF WEEK	MORNING		AFTERNOON		OVERTIME		FOR OFFICE USE ONLY	
	IN	OUT	IN	OUT	IN	OUT	REGULAR HOURS	OVERTIME HOURS
MONDAY								
TUESDAY								
WEDNESDAY								
THURSDAY								
FRIDAY								
SATURDAY								
SUNDAY								
TOTAL HOURS								

OVERTIME AUTHORIZATION_____ EMPLOYEE SIGNATURE_____

This time sheet must be filled and signed by Employee Daily .
Overtime needs to be authorized by Authority First.

Weekly Time Sheet

EMPLOYEE NAME:		WEEK ENDING:
DEPARTMENT:		EXEMPTIONS:

DAY OF WEEK	MORNING		AFTERNOON		OVERTIME		FOR OFFICE USE ONLY	
	IN	OUT	IN	OUT	IN	OUT	REGULAR HOURS	OVERTIME HOURS
MONDAY								
TUESDAY								
WEDNESDAY								
THURSDAY								
FRIDAY								
SATURDAY								
SUNDAY								
TOTAL HOURS								

OVERTIME
AUTHORIZATION_____

EMPLOYEE
SIGNATURE_____

This time sheet must be filled and signed by Employee Daily .
Overtime needs to be authorized by Authority First.

Weekly Time Sheet

EMPLOYEE NAME:

WEEK ENDING:

DEPARTMENT:

EXEMPTIONS:

DAY OF WEEK	MORNING		AFTERNOON		OVERTIME		FOR OFFICE USE ONLY	
	IN	OUT	IN	OUT	IN	OUT	REGULAR HOURS	OVERTIME HOURS
MONDAY								
TUESDAY								
WEDNESDAY								
THURSDAY								
FRIDAY								
SATURDAY								
SUNDAY								
TOTAL HOURS								

OVERTIME AUTHORIZATION_____

EMPLOYEE SIGNATURE_____

This time sheet must be filled and signed by Employee Daily .
Overtime needs to be authorized by Authority First.

Weekly Time Sheet

EMPLOYEE NAME:	WEEK ENDING:
DEPARTMENT:	EXEMPTIONS:

DAY OF WEEK	MORNING		AFTERNOON		OVERTIME		FOR OFFICE USE ONLY	
	IN	OUT	IN	OUT	IN	OUT	REGULAR HOURS	OVERTIME HOURS
MONDAY								
TUESDAY								
WEDNESDAY								
THURSDAY								
FRIDAY								
SATURDAY								
SUNDAY								
TOTAL HOURS								

OVERTIME
AUTHORIZATION_____

EMPLOYEE
SIGNATURE_____

This time sheet must be filled and signed by Employee Daily .
Overtime needs to be authorized by Authority First.

Weekly Time Sheet

EMPLOYEE NAME:		WEEK ENDING:
DEPARTMENT:		EXEMPTIONS:

DAY OF WEEK	MORNING		AFTERNOON		OVERTIME		FOR OFFICE USE ONLY	
	IN	OUT	IN	OUT	IN	OUT	REGULAR HOURS	OVERTIME HOURS
MONDAY								
TUESDAY								
WEDNESDAY								
THURSDAY								
FRIDAY								
SATURDAY								
SUNDAY								
TOTAL HOURS								

OVERTIME
AUTHORIZATION_____

EMPLOYEE
SIGNATURE_____

This time sheet must be filled and signed by Employee Daily .
Overtime needs to be authorized by Authority First.

Weekly Time Sheet

EMPLOYEE NAME:	WEEK ENDING:
DEPARTMENT:	EXEMPTIONS:

DAY OF WEEK	MORNING		AFTERNOON		OVERTIME		FOR OFFICE USE ONLY	
	IN	OUT	IN	OUT	IN	OUT	REGULAR HOURS	OVERTIME HOURS
MONDAY								
TUESDAY								
WEDNESDAY								
THURSDAY								
FRIDAY								
SATURDAY								
SUNDAY								
TOTAL HOURS								

OVERTIME
AUTHORIZATION_____

EMPLOYEE
SIGNATURE_____

This time sheet must be filled and signed by Employee Daily .
Overtime needs to be authorized by Authority First.

Weekly Time Sheet

| EMPLOYEE NAME: | | WEEK ENDING: |
| DEPARTMENT: | | EXEMPTIONS: |

DAY OF WEEK	MORNING		AFTERNOON		OVERTIME		FOR OFFICE USE ONLY	
	IN	OUT	IN	OUT	IN	OUT	REGULAR HOURS	OVERTIME HOURS
MONDAY								
TUESDAY								
WEDNESDAY								
THURSDAY								
FRIDAY								
SATURDAY								
SUNDAY								
TOTAL HOURS								

OVERTIME
AUTHORIZATION_____

EMPLOYEE
SIGNATURE_____

This time sheet must be filled and signed by Employee Daily .
Overtime needs to be authorized by Authority First.

Weekly Time Sheet

EMPLOYEE NAME:	WEEK ENDING:
DEPARTMENT:	EXEMPTIONS:

DAY OF WEEK	MORNING		AFTERNOON		OVERTIME		FOR OFFICE USE ONLY	
	IN	OUT	IN	OUT	IN	OUT	REGULAR HOURS	OVERTIME HOURS
MONDAY								
TUESDAY								
WEDNESDAY								
THURSDAY								
FRIDAY								
SATURDAY								
SUNDAY								
TOTAL HOURS								

OVERTIME
AUTHORIZATION_____

EMPLOYEE
SIGNATURE_____

This time sheet must be filled and signed by Employee Daily .
Overtime needs to be authorized by Authority First.

Weekly Time Sheet

| EMPLOYEE NAME: | | WEEK ENDING: |
| DEPARTMENT: | | EXEMPTIONS: |

DAY OF WEEK	MORNING		AFTERNOON		OVERTIME		FOR OFFICE USE ONLY	
	IN	OUT	IN	OUT	IN	OUT	REGULAR HOURS	OVERTIME HOURS
MONDAY								
TUESDAY								
WEDNESDAY								
THURSDAY								
FRIDAY								
SATURDAY								
SUNDAY								
TOTAL HOURS								

OVERTIME
AUTHORIZATION_____

EMPLOYEE
SIGNATURE_____

This time sheet must be filled and signed by Employee Daily .
Overtime needs to be authorized by Authority First.

Weekly Time Sheet

EMPLOYEE NAME:		WEEK ENDING:
DEPARTMENT:		EXEMPTIONS:

DAY OF WEEK	MORNING		AFTERNOON		OVERTIME		FOR OFFICE USE ONLY	
	IN	OUT	IN	OUT	IN	OUT	REGULAR HOURS	OVERTIME HOURS
MONDAY								
TUESDAY								
WEDNESDAY								
THURSDAY								
FRIDAY								
SATURDAY								
SUNDAY								
TOTAL HOURS								

OVERTIME AUTHORIZATION_____

EMPLOYEE SIGNATURE_____

This time sheet must be filled and signed by Employee Daily .
Overtime needs to be authorized by Authority First.

Weekly Time Sheet

EMPLOYEE NAME:		WEEK ENDING:
DEPARTMENT:		EXEMPTIONS:

DAY OF WEEK	MORNING		AFTERNOON		OVERTIME		FOR OFFICE USE ONLY	
	IN	OUT	IN	OUT	IN	OUT	REGULAR HOURS	OVERTIME HOURS
MONDAY								
TUESDAY								
WEDNESDAY								
THURSDAY								
FRIDAY								
SATURDAY								
SUNDAY								
TOTAL HOURS								

OVERTIME AUTHORIZATION_____ EMPLOYEE SIGNATURE_____

This time sheet must be filled and signed by Employee Daily .
Overtime needs to be authorized by Authority First.

Weekly Time Sheet

EMPLOYEE NAME:	WEEK ENDING:
DEPARTMENT:	EXEMPTIONS:

DAY OF WEEK	MORNING		AFTERNOON		OVERTIME		FOR OFFICE USE ONLY	
	IN	OUT	IN	OUT	IN	OUT	REGULAR HOURS	OVERTIME HOURS
MONDAY								
TUESDAY								
WEDNESDAY								
THURSDAY								
FRIDAY								
SATURDAY								
SUNDAY								
TOTAL HOURS								

OVERTIME
AUTHORIZATION_____

EMPLOYEE
SIGNATURE_____

This time sheet must be filled and signed by Employee Daily .
Overtime needs to be authorized by Authority First.

Weekly Time Sheet

EMPLOYEE NAME:	WEEK ENDING:
DEPARTMENT:	EXEMPTIONS:

DAY OF WEEK	MORNING		AFTERNOON		OVERTIME		FOR OFFICE USE ONLY	
	IN	OUT	IN	OUT	IN	OUT	REGULAR HOURS	OVERTIME HOURS
MONDAY								
TUESDAY								
WEDNESDAY								
THURSDAY								
FRIDAY								
SATURDAY								
SUNDAY								
TOTAL HOURS								

OVERTIME
AUTHORIZATION_____

EMPLOYEE
SIGNATURE_____

This time sheet must be filled and signed by Employee Daily .
Overtime needs to be authorized by Authority First.

Weekly Time Sheet

EMPLOYEE NAME:	WEEK ENDING:
DEPARTMENT:	EXEMPTIONS:

DAY OF WEEK	MORNING		AFTERNOON		OVERTIME		FOR OFFICE USE ONLY	
	IN	OUT	IN	OUT	IN	OUT	REGULAR HOURS	OVERTIME HOURS
MONDAY								
TUESDAY								
WEDNESDAY								
THURSDAY								
FRIDAY								
SATURDAY								
SUNDAY								
TOTAL HOURS								

OVERTIME AUTHORIZATION_____

EMPLOYEE SIGNATURE_____

This time sheet must be filled and signed by Employee Daily .
Overtime needs to be authorized by Authority First.

Weekly Time Sheet

EMPLOYEE NAME:	WEEK ENDING:
DEPARTMENT:	EXEMPTIONS:

DAY OF WEEK	MORNING		AFTERNOON		OVERTIME		FOR OFFICE USE ONLY	
	IN	OUT	IN	OUT	IN	OUT	REGULAR HOURS	OVERTIME HOURS
MONDAY								
TUESDAY								
WEDNESDAY								
THURSDAY								
FRIDAY								
SATURDAY								
SUNDAY								
TOTAL HOURS								

OVERTIME
AUTHORIZATION_____

EMPLOYEE
SIGNATURE_____

This time sheet must be filled and signed by Employee Daily .
Overtime needs to be authorized by Authority First.

Weekly Time Sheet

EMPLOYEE NAME:		WEEK ENDING:
DEPARTMENT:		EXEMPTIONS:

DAY OF WEEK	MORNING		AFTERNOON		OVERTIME		FOR OFFICE USE ONLY	
	IN	OUT	IN	OUT	IN	OUT	REGULAR HOURS	OVERTIME HOURS
MONDAY								
TUESDAY								
WEDNESDAY								
THURSDAY								
FRIDAY								
SATURDAY								
SUNDAY								
TOTAL HOURS								

OVERTIME
AUTHORIZATION_____

EMPLOYEE
SIGNATURE_____

This time sheet must be filled and signed by Employee Daily .
Overtime needs to be authorized by Authority First.

Weekly Time Sheet

| EMPLOYEE NAME: | | WEEK ENDING: |
| DEPARTMENT: | | EXEMPTIONS: |

DAY OF WEEK	MORNING		AFTERNOON		OVERTIME		FOR OFFICE USE ONLY	
	IN	OUT	IN	OUT	IN	OUT	REGULAR HOURS	OVERTIME HOURS
MONDAY								
TUESDAY								
WEDNESDAY								
THURSDAY								
FRIDAY								
SATURDAY								
SUNDAY								
TOTAL HOURS								

OVERTIME AUTHORIZATION_____ EMPLOYEE SIGNATURE_____

This time sheet must be filled and signed by Employee Daily .
Overtime needs to be authorized by Authority First.

Weekly Time Sheet

EMPLOYEE NAME:	WEEK ENDING:
DEPARTMENT:	EXEMPTIONS:

DAY OF WEEK	MORNING		AFTERNOON		OVERTIME		FOR OFFICE USE ONLY	
	IN	OUT	IN	OUT	IN	OUT	REGULAR HOURS	OVERTIME HOURS
MONDAY								
TUESDAY								
WEDNESDAY								
THURSDAY								
FRIDAY								
SATURDAY								
SUNDAY								
TOTAL HOURS								

OVERTIME
AUTHORIZATION_____

EMPLOYEE
SIGNATURE_____

This time sheet must be filled and signed by Employee Daily .
Overtime needs to be authorized by Authority First.

Weekly Time Sheet

EMPLOYEE NAME:	WEEK ENDING:
DEPARTMENT:	EXEMPTIONS:

DAY OF WEEK	MORNING		AFTERNOON		OVERTIME		FOR OFFICE USE ONLY	
	IN	OUT	IN	OUT	IN	OUT	REGULAR HOURS	OVERTIME HOURS
MONDAY								
TUESDAY								
WEDNESDAY								
THURSDAY								
FRIDAY								
SATURDAY								
SUNDAY								
TOTAL HOURS								

OVERTIME
AUTHORIZATION_____

EMPLOYEE
SIGNATURE_____

This time sheet must be filled and signed by Employee Daily .
Overtime needs to be authorized by Authority First.

Weekly Time Sheet

EMPLOYEE NAME:	WEEK ENDING:
DEPARTMENT:	EXEMPTIONS:

DAY OF WEEK	MORNING		AFTERNOON		OVERTIME		FOR OFFICE USE ONLY	
	IN	OUT	IN	OUT	IN	OUT	REGULAR HOURS	OVERTIME HOURS
MONDAY								
TUESDAY								
WEDNESDAY								
THURSDAY								
FRIDAY								
SATURDAY								
SUNDAY								
TOTAL HOURS								

OVERTIME
AUTHORIZATION_____

EMPLOYEE
SIGNATURE_____

This time sheet must be filled and signed by Employee Daily .
Overtime needs to be authorized by Authority First.

Weekly Time Sheet

EMPLOYEE NAME:	WEEK ENDING:
DEPARTMENT:	EXEMPTIONS:

DAY OF WEEK	MORNING		AFTERNOON		OVERTIME		FOR OFFICE USE ONLY	
	IN	OUT	IN	OUT	IN	OUT	REGULAR HOURS	OVERTIME HOURS
MONDAY								
TUESDAY								
WEDNESDAY								
THURSDAY								
FRIDAY								
SATURDAY								
SUNDAY								
TOTAL HOURS								

OVERTIME
AUTHORIZATION_____

EMPLOYEE
SIGNATURE_____

**This time sheet must be filled and signed by Employee Daily .
Overtime needs to be authorized by Authority First.**

Weekly Time Sheet

EMPLOYEE NAME:	WEEK ENDING:
DEPARTMENT:	EXEMPTIONS:

DAY OF WEEK	MORNING		AFTERNOON		OVERTIME		FOR OFFICE USE ONLY	
	IN	OUT	IN	OUT	IN	OUT	REGULAR HOURS	OVERTIME HOURS
MONDAY								
TUESDAY								
WEDNESDAY								
THURSDAY								
FRIDAY								
SATURDAY								
SUNDAY								
TOTAL HOURS								

OVERTIME AUTHORIZATION_____

EMPLOYEE SIGNATURE_____

This time sheet must be filled and signed by Employee Daily .
Overtime needs to be authorized by Authority First.

Weekly Time Sheet

EMPLOYEE NAME: WEEK ENDING:

DEPARTMENT: EXEMPTIONS:

DAY OF WEEK	MORNING		AFTERNOON		OVERTIME		FOR OFFICE USE ONLY	
	IN	OUT	IN	OUT	IN	OUT	REGULAR HOURS	OVERTIME HOURS
MONDAY								
TUESDAY								
WEDNESDAY								
THURSDAY								
FRIDAY								
SATURDAY								
SUNDAY								
TOTAL HOURS								

OVERTIME
AUTHORIZATION_____

EMPLOYEE
SIGNATURE_____

This time sheet must be filled and signed by Employee Daily .
Overtime needs to be authorized by Authority First.

Weekly Time Sheet

EMPLOYEE NAME:	WEEK ENDING:
DEPARTMENT:	EXEMPTIONS:

DAY OF WEEK	MORNING		AFTERNOON		OVERTIME		FOR OFFICE USE ONLY	
	IN	OUT	IN	OUT	IN	OUT	REGULAR HOURS	OVERTIME HOURS
MONDAY								
TUESDAY								
WEDNESDAY								
THURSDAY								
FRIDAY								
SATURDAY								
SUNDAY								
TOTAL HOURS								

OVERTIME
AUTHORIZATION_____

EMPLOYEE
SIGNATURE_____

This time sheet must be filled and signed by Employee Daily .
Overtime needs to be authorized by Authority First.

Weekly Time Sheet

EMPLOYEE NAME:		WEEK ENDING:	
DEPARTMENT:		EXEMPTIONS:	

DAY OF WEEK	MORNING		AFTERNOON		OVERTIME		FOR OFFICE USE ONLY	
	IN	OUT	IN	OUT	IN	OUT	REGULAR HOURS	OVERTIME HOURS
MONDAY								
TUESDAY								
WEDNESDAY								
THURSDAY								
FRIDAY								
SATURDAY								
SUNDAY								
TOTAL HOURS								

OVERTIME AUTHORIZATION_____   **EMPLOYEE SIGNATURE**_____

This time sheet must be filled and signed by Employee Daily .
Overtime needs to be authorized by Authority First.

Weekly Time Sheet

EMPLOYEE NAME:	WEEK ENDING:
DEPARTMENT:	EXEMPTIONS:

DAY OF WEEK	MORNING		AFTERNOON		OVERTIME		FOR OFFICE USE ONLY	
	IN	OUT	IN	OUT	IN	OUT	REGULAR HOURS	OVERTIME HOURS
MONDAY								
TUESDAY								
WEDNESDAY								
THURSDAY								
FRIDAY								
SATURDAY								
SUNDAY								
TOTAL HOURS								

OVERTIME AUTHORIZATION_____

EMPLOYEE SIGNATURE_____

This time sheet must be filled and signed by Employee Daily .
Overtime needs to be authorized by Authority First.

Weekly Time Sheet

EMPLOYEE NAME:	WEEK ENDING:
DEPARTMENT:	EXEMPTIONS:

DAY OF WEEK	MORNING		AFTERNOON		OVERTIME		FOR OFFICE USE ONLY	
	IN	OUT	IN	OUT	IN	OUT	REGULAR HOURS	OVERTIME HOURS
MONDAY								
TUESDAY								
WEDNESDAY								
THURSDAY								
FRIDAY								
SATURDAY								
SUNDAY								
TOTAL HOURS								

OVERTIME
AUTHORIZATION_____

EMPLOYEE
SIGNATURE_____

This time sheet must be filled and signed by Employee Daily .
Overtime needs to be authorized by Authority First.

NOTES

NOTES

Made in the USA
Monee, IL
07 November 2022

17313119R00070